LUSH LIFE

First published in 2005 by Oberon Books Ltd
521 Caledonian Road, London N7 9RH
Tel: 020 7607 3637 / Fax: 020 7607 3629
e-mail: oberon.books@btconnect.com
www.oberonbooks.com

A catalogue record for this book is available from the British Library.

Every effort has been made to track down the copyright holders of the song lyrics printed in this book.

ISBN: 1 84002 561 1

Cover design: Blue River
Cover photography: Critical Tortoise

Characters

HANNAH 'LOTTE' HANWAY

COP

LOTTE is played by five actress/singers, each of whom represents a different aspect of the same woman. In the text the different parts are numbered 1, 2, 3, 4 and 5. The COP is played by one actress.

Script Note

The spoken text for the five actress/singers playing LOTTE is arranged musically and should be read from left to right in the same way a musician would read a score written for a quintet.

Songs

Songs should be divided between the five actress/singers, apart from those marked in the text as sung by the COP.

For Natalie, Joe and Elena

Special thanks to Max Roberts.
Gratitude and thanks also to Alan Plater, Cleo Laine,
Tracy Gillman and all at Live Theatre.

ACT ONE

A Nightclub.

LUSH LIFE

Music & Lyrics: Billy Strayhorn

I USED TO VISIT ALL THE VERY GAY PLACES
THOSE COME WHAT MAY PLACES
WHERE ONE RELAXES ON THE AXIS
OF THE WHEEL OF LIFE
TO GET THE FEEL OF LIFE
FROM JAZZ AND COCKTAILS

THE GIRLS I KNEW HAD SAD AND SULLEN GREY FACES
WITH DISTINGUÉ TRACES
THAT USED TO BE THERE
YOU COULD SEE WHERE
THEY'D BEEN WASHED AWAY
BY TOO MANY THROUGH THE DAY
TWELVE O'CLOCK TAILS

THEN YOU CAME ALONG
WITH YOUR SIREN SONG
TO TEMPT ME TO MADNESS
I THOUGHT FOR A WHILE
THAT YOUR POIGNANT SMILE
WAS TINGED WITH A SADNESS
OF A GREAT LOVE FOR ME

OH YES I WAS WRONG AGAIN
I WAS WRONG

LIFE IS LONELY AGAIN
AND ONLY LAST YEAR
EVERYTHING SEEMED SO SURE

NOW LIFE IS AWFUL AGAIN
A DRAWER FULL OF ART
COULD ONLY BE A BORE

A WEEK IN PARIS
WILL EASE THE BITE OF IT
ALL I CARE IS TO SMILE
IN SPITE OF IT

I'LL FORGET YOU I WILL
WHILE YET YOU ARE STILL
BURNING INSIDE
MY BRAIN

ROMANCE IS MUSH
STIFLING THOSE WHO STRIVE
I'LL LIVE A LUSH LIFE
IN SOME SMALL DIVE
AND THERE I'LL THINK
WHILE I ROT
WITH THE REST
OF THOSE WHOSE LIVES ARE LONELY TOO

1   I used to associate people who hung around in bars drinking till the early
2
3
4
5

1	hours of the morning with glamour. Now I just associate it with headaches			
2				
3			headaches	
4			headaches	
5				

1			Booze	
2	Piano bars	Clubs		
3			Dives	
4		Pubs		Smoke
5		Wine bars		God, the smoke

1			What?	
2		Wasn't that bad	I packed it in	
3			What?	
4	Me throat, some nights		What?	I'm talking
5			What?	

1		
2		
3		Packed it in! Up all night smoking and drinking
4	about passive smoking	
5		

1		That was different
2		Me first
3	coffee and going on about packing it in!	
4		
5		

1	
2	cigarette in six months
3	Big deal
4	Anyway, like I say, I was talking about
5	

1	
2	
3	
4	passive smoking · Ex-agent
5	You can sue for that, you know. My agent –

1	
2	
3	
4	
5	My ex-agent was going to sue some club somewhere. One of his turns got

1	Sam and Jeff the Giraffe
2	Jeff the Giraffe
3	Jeff the Giraffe. He was
4	emphysema · Jeff the Giraffe
5	emphysema. Ventriloquist. Sideways Sam and Jeff the Giraffe

1	Takes me back
2	I don't smoke
3	shite · Except for last night
4	Bless him · And
5	

1
2   OK – apart from last night and the occasional joint, I
3
4 the occasional joint
5

1
2 don't smoke. And I don't drink   Which isn't that often
3   Except when I do
4
5

1 Not these days
2   Chocolate
3   Shopping
4   Got plenty of other vices, mind
5

1   Men
2   Men. Men   No   No, not before
3   Men   Bastards   Bastards. Even before him
4 Shoes. Men
5   Men

1
2
3 Come off it   Don't be stupid   Nothing
4   It was my fault
5   I did nothing wrong. Nothing

1	Men	Cheers (*Drinks.*) Me Mam was a drinker. Bacardi
2		Cheers (*Drinks.*)
3	Why do we bother? Cheers (*Drinks.*)	
4		Cheers (*Drinks.*)
5		Cheers (*Drinks.*)

1		One
2		She didn't
3		Used to pour it on her Frosties
4	First thing in the morning	
5		

1	of me Dad's jokes	
2		
3		Drunk as sin by the middle of the afternoon, though
4		
5		

1		
2		
3	Used to come home from school and there she'd be, draped over the	
4		
5		

1		
2		
3	stereo, out for the count, half way through putting an LP on, or taking it off	
4		
5		

1	
2	It was
3	Why? It's the truth
4	You don't need to tell people that I know, but –
5	

1	
2	Mam introduced us to Ella. Ella Fitzgerald – the First Lady of Song. 'My
3	
4	
5	

1	'Blue Moon'
2	Funny Valentine'
3	'I Can't Give
4	'Love For Sale'
5	'Here In My Arms'

1	(Sings.) YOU ANYTHING BUT LOVE'
2	(Sings.) YOU ANYTHING BUT LOVE'
3	(Sings.) YOU ANYTHING BUT LOVE'
4	(Sings.) YOU ANYTHING BUT LOVE'
5	(Sings.) YOU ANYTHING BUT LOVE, BABY, LOVE'S THE ONLY THING

1	All on the Verve
2	78s, singles, LPs
3	All Right, all right…
4	
5	I'M THINKING OF, BABY'

1	label	Cheers *(Drinks.)* It's only water. Have you ever been to Los
2		Cheers *(Drinks.)* It's only water.
3	Christ…	Cheers *(Drinks.)*
4		Cheers *(Drinks.)*
5		Cheers *(Drinks.)*

1	Angeles?
2	
3	What a place
4	I wish I'd never set eyes on it
5	It's fantastic, don't listen

1	I went to Inglewood Park Cemetery
2	The Sanctuary of the Bells
3	
4	
5	to her

1	
2	Where Ella is I knew you'd say that
3	Bit of an anti-climax
4	To her grave
5	

1	
2	
3	Well, it was
4	
5	

BLACK COFFEE

Music & Lyrics: Paul Francis Webster & Sonny Burke

I'M FEELIN' MIGHTY LONESOME
HAVEN'T SLEPT A WINK
I WALK THE FLOOR AN' WATCH THE DOOR
IN BETWEEN I DRINK
BLACK COFFEE …

LOVE'S A HAND-ME-DOWN BREW
I'LL NEVER KNOW A SUNDAY
IN THIS WEEKDAY ROOM

I'M TALKIN' TO THE SHADOWS
ONE O'CLOCK TO FOUR
AND LORD HOW SLOW THE MOMENTS GO
WHEN ALL I DO IS POUR
BLACK COFFEE …

SINCE THE BLUES CAUGHT MY EYE
I'M HANGIN' OUT ON MONDAY
MY SUNDAY DREAMS TO DRY

NOW A MAN IS BORN TO GO A-LOVING
A WOMAN'S BORN TO WEEP AND FRET
TO STAY AT HOME AND BE ALONE
AND DROWN HER PAST REGRETS
IN COFFEE AND CIGARETTES

I'M MOONIN' ALL THE MORNIN'
MOURNIN' ALL THE NIGHT
AND IN BETWEEN IT'S NICOTINE
AND NOT MUCH HEART TO FIGHT
BLACK COFFEE …

FEELIN' LOW AS THE GROUND

It's driving me crazy
This waitin' for my baby
To maybe come around

My nerves have gone to pieces
My hair is turning grey
All I do is drink black coffee
Since my man's gone away

Lights up. Inglewood Police Department. COP writing a report.

COP: Friend of mine got killed about a week back. Captain Walsh, twenty-five year veteran, served in the Robbery and Assaults Section, Patrol Bureau, Homicide Unit and Narcotics Division. Seen things you wouldn't believe. All that and he gets killed in a traffic accident on his way to pick up his wife from the Mall. Some guy runs a red light. Walsh swerves to avoid a collision and BAM! – straight into an oncoming truck. So what do we do? We step up the City's Red Light Photo Enforcement Program and set up a drivers' licence checkpoint in the area of La Brea and Florence Avenue. You better watch out you don't get stopped driving drunk or without a valid licence. The funeral was yesterday – Inglewood Park Cemetery. It was the last place I wanted to go back to today.

Lights down.

1	My name is a palindrome. Hannah. H-a-n-n-a-h. It spells the same
2	Hannah. H-a-n-n-a-h
3	Hannah. H-a-n-n-a-h
4	Hannah. H-a-n-n-a-h
5	Hannah. H-a-n-n-a-h

1	backwards as it does forwards. Like Oxo. Or 'Able was I ere I saw Elba'
2	ere I saw Elba'
3	ere I saw Elba'
4	ere I saw Elba'
5	ere I saw Elba'

1	Me Dad taught us that
2	Me first boyfriend, Don, didn't like me name
3	God help us
4	
5	

1	
2	Would you stop interrupting? Don didn't like me name So he
3	Prat
4	
5	

1	And it stuck
2	decided to call us Lotte
3	
4	
5	That's my professional name. Lotte.

1	
2	I met Don when I was still
3	
4	But my real name is Hannah
5	Lotte Hanway

1	Something like that
2	at school. Carpet fitter I was fifteen. It was fate
3	Prat You what!
4	Huh!
5	

1	
2	We went out for eleven months
3	Then he finished with us
4	I was so shy
5	

1	Bloody hell that hurt
2	
3	Don't be ridiculous
4	I thought I was going to die
5	What?

1	
2	I did Didn't know what to do with
3	
4	I did Cried and cried and cried
5	Give over

1	
2	meself
3	No
4	I actually contemplated suicide Seriously. I did. I took an
5	No

1	
2	Sort of
3	Overdose!
4	overdose I did
5	Don't be such a drama queen Eleven Junior

1	
2	I made meself throw up
3	Nothing happened
4	I was serious!
5	Disprin!

1	
2	
3	
4	Never told no one that before…
5	

I GOT IT BAD (AND THAT AIN'T GOOD)

Lyrics: Paul Francis Webster   *Music: Duke Ellington*

THE POETS SAY THAT ALL WHO LOVE ARE BLIND
BUT I'M IN LOVE AND I KNOW WHAT TIME IT IS
THE GOOD BOOK SAYS GO SEEK AND YE SHALL FIND
WELL, I HAVE SOUGHT AND MY WHAT A CLIMB IT IS

MY LIFE IS JUST LIKE THE WEATHER
IT CHANGES WTH THE HOURS
WHEN HE'S NEAR I'M FAIR AND WARMER
WHEN HE'S GONE I'M CLOUDY WITH SHOWERS

And motion like the ocean
It's either sink or swim
When a woman loves a man
Like i love him

Never treats me sweet and gentle
The way he should
I got it bad and that ain't good

My poor heart is sentimental
Not made of wood
I got it bad and that ain't good
But when the weekend's over
I end up like i started out
Just cryin' my lil' heart out
He don't love me
Like i love him
No, nobody could
I got it bad and that ain't good
So bad, so bad
I got it bad, so bad

Though folks with good intentions
Tell me to save my tears
I'm glad
I'm mad about you
Lord above me
Make him love me
The way he should
Like a lonely weeping willow lost in the wood
The things i tell my pillow
No woman should
I got it bad, and that ain't good

1		Spiky hair
2	Then there was Terry	
3		
4		Terry Larsen
5		Thought he was Mick Ronson

1	Guitarist, Spiders From Mars, David Bowie	
2		
3		Used to wear one of his Mam's
4		
5		

1	God, he was cute	
2		I don't know
3	lurex blouses	
4		I don't know
5	I treated him like shite	

1		But
2	why. He was a lot nicer than Don	
3		
4	why	He would've done anything for us
5		

1	the harder he tried the worse I treated him	Power
2		Power
3	Couldn't stop meself.	Power
4		Power
5	the worse I treated him	Power

1	I had power	
2		
3	'Terry, get us a drink'	And he
4		
5	'Terry, take us to the pictures'	

1	Never complained	
2		
3	did	Right where I wanted
4		
5	Had him under the proverbial	

1	No challenge	
2		
3	him	You don't want it do you – someone
4		
5	So I packed him in	

1		Then
2	Begged me to take him back	
3	trying that hard	The works
4	Begged me to take him back	
5	Begged me to take him back. Tears	

1	he met this manicurist and went to live in Berwick	I was…
2		I was…
3		
4		When
5		

1	
2	
3	
4	I could have him, I didn't want him, when I couldn't have him, I did
5	

1	Nothing doing
2	I tried to get him back
3	Typical
4	He wasn't stupid
5	

YOU TURNED THE TABLES ON ME

Lyrics: Sidney D Mitchell   *Music: Louis Alter*

I USED TO BE THE APPLE OF YOUR EYE
I HAD YOU WITH ME EVERY DAY,
BUT NOW WHENEVER YOU ARE PASSING BY
YOU'RE ALWAYS LOOKING THE OTHER WAY
IT'S LITTLE THINGS LIKE THIS
THAT PROMPT ME TO SAY:

YOU TURNED THE TABLES ON ME
AND NOW I'M FALLING FOR YOU;
YOU TURNED THE TABLES ON ME
I CAN'T BELIEVE THAT IT'S TRUE
I ALWAYS THOUGHT WHEN YOU BROUGHT
THE LOVELY PRESENT YOU BOUGHT
WHY HADN'T YOU BROUGHT ME MORE,
BUT NOW IF YOU'D COME
I'D WELCOME ANYTHING

FROM THE FIVE AND TEN CENT STORE,
YOU USED TO CALL ME THE TOP
YOU PUT ME UP ON A THRONE
YOU LET ME FALL WITH A DROP
AND NOW I'M OUT ON MY OWN.
BUT AFTER THINKING IT OVER AND OVER,
I GOT WHAT WAS COMING TO ME
JUST LIKE THE STING OF A BEE
YOU TURNED THE TABLES ON ME.

1	And that was that	I sometimes wonder what might
2	Never saw him again	
3		
4	Never saw him again	
5		

1	have been	Do you know how to mix the perfect
2		
3	But we'll never know	
4		
5		

1	Bloody Mary?	Two parts vodka, three parts tomato juice, six dashes of
2		Two parts vodka, three parts tomato juice, six dashes of
3		Two parts vodka, three parts tomato juice, six dashes of
4		Two parts vodka, three parts tomato juice, six dashes of
5		Two parts vodka, three parts tomato juice, six dashes of

1	Worcestershire sauce, five dashes of tabasco, dash of lemon juice, salt
2	Worcestershire sauce, five dashes of tabasco, dash of lemon juice, salt
3	Worcestershire sauce, five dashes of tabasco, dash of lemon juice, salt
4	Worcestershire sauce, five dashes of tabasco, dash of lemon juice, salt
5	Worcestershire sauce, five dashes of tabasco, dash of lemon juice, salt

1	and pepper. Mam showed us	
2	and pepper	Come
3	and pepper	
4	and pepper	I had to mix one for her every night
5	and pepper	

1	
2	off it
3	Near enough every night
4	Near enough every night
5	If we didn't have Worcestershire sauce

1	
2	
3	
4	I'm
5	or tabasco I'd put Brown sauce in… she never seemed to notice

1	
2	That's why I don't drink or smoke any more
3	
4	diabetic
5	Ella was diabetic

1

2 It came on in me thirties

3

4   I've got a cataract in me left eye. It's like looking

5

1

2

3   Lord

4 through a mist all the time. I'm supposed to be having an operation

5

1

2

3 knows when

4   I'm also prone to corns, bunions and styes, so if you see us

5

1

2

3

4 walking down the Shields Road in Dr Scholl sandals and dark glasses

5

---

1   I suppose I better tell you about Michael…

2   Michael

3   About time

4 you know why   No

5   Why?

1 I was doing this gig

2

3

4   Semi-pro.

5   I do this professionally, you know, the singing

1

2

3

4 Don't earn much

5   What you talking like that for? Don't listen to her. I may

1

2

3

4

5 not be at the peak of me career right now, but that doesn't mean I don't

1

2

3

4

5 have a professional attitude and it doesn't mean I'm not bloody good. I have

1

2

3

4

5 toured all over the UK. I have recorded two solo albums. I am not semi-pro.

1	
2	
3	
4	
5	I deserve to be taken seriously. I work bloody hard, unlike some of these

1	
2	
3	
4	
5	Pop Idols off the tele… I just didn't get the break, that's all. I should have

1	
2	
3	
4	
5	had more success. But I'll get there. I will. One day. You just watch me!

1	Anyway, I was doing this gig
2	Hotel. Piano
3	She's right
4	Finished?
5	

1	
2	bar. Cole Porter, Duke, Billy Strayhorn, Rogers & Hart – Ella songs mostly.
3	
4	
5	

1	And there he was		
2	there he was. Stood at the bar		
3	there he was	Eyes glued to us	
4	there he was		
5	there he was		I was looking good

1		Very smart	
2	He was wearing a suit	Very smart. Very well groomed	
3			
4		Very well groomed	
5	Tailored	Very well groomed. Not a hair	

1		so good looking	
2	And so good looking		But very good looking.
3		Bit of a shortarse	
4		so good looking	
5	out of place	so good looking	

1			Anyway,
2	You could tell he'd smell nice		But he wasn't
3		I thought he was gay	
4			
5		gay	

1	he caught me eye. I smiled, he smiled…
2	
3	
4	
5	

THIS COULD BE THE START OF SOMETHING BIG

Music & Lyrics: Steve Allen

YOU'RE WALKING ALONG THE STREET
OR YOU'RE AT A PARTY
OR ELSE YOU'RE ALONE AND THEN YOU SUDDENLY DIG
YOU'RE LOOKING IN SOMEONE'S EYES YOU SUDDENLY REALISE
THAT THIS COULD BE THE START OF SOMETHING BIG

YOU'RE LUNCHING AT TWENTY-ONE AND WATCHING YOUR DIET
DECLINING A CHARLOTTE RUSSE, ACCEPTING A FIG
WHEN OUT OF THE CLEAR BLUE SKY YOU'RE SUDDENLY GAL AND
    GUY
AND THIS COULD BE THE START OF SOMETHING BIG

THERE'S NO CONTROLLING THE UNROLLING OF YOUR FATE MY
    FRIEND
WHO KNOWS WHAT'S WRITTEN IN THE MAGIC BOOK
BUT WHEN A LOVER YOU DISCOVER AT THE GATE MY FRIEND
INVITE HIM IN WITHOUT A SECOND LOOK

YOU'RE UP IN AN AEROPLANE OR DINING AT SARDI'S
OR LYING AT MALIBU ALONE ON THE SAND
YOU SUDDENLY HEAR A BELL AND RIGHT AWAY YOU CAN TELL
THAT THIS COULD BE THE START OF SOMETHING GRAND

YOU'RE DOING YOUR INCOME TAX OR BUYING A TOOTHBRUSH
OR HURRYING HOME BECAUSE THE HOUR IS LATE
THEN SUDDENLY THERE YOU GO THE VERY NEXT THING YOU
    KNOW
IS THIS COULD BE THE START OF SOMETHING GREAT

YOU'RE HAVING A SNOWBALL FIGHT OR PICKING UP DAISIES
YOU'RE SINGING A HAPPY TUNE OR KNOCKING ON WOOD
WHEN ALL OF A SUDDEN YOU

LOOK UP AND THERE'S SOMETHING NEW
OH THIS COULD BE THE START OF SOMETHING GOOD

YOUR DESTINED LOVER YOU DISCOVER IN A LIGHTNING FLASH
SO KEEP YOUR HEART AWAKE BOTH NIGHT AND DAY
BECAUSE THE MEETING MAY BE FLEETING AS THE LIGHTNING FLASH
AND YOU DON'T WANT TO LET IT SLIP AWAY

YOU'RE WATCHING THE SUN COME UP OR COUNTING YOUR
        MONEY
OR ELSE IN A DIM CAFE YOU'RE ORDERING WINE
THEN SUDDENLY THERE HE IS YOU WANNA BE WHERE HE IS
AND THIS MUST BE THE START OF SOMETHING
THIS COULD BE THE HEART OF SOMETHING
THIS COULD BE THE START OF SOMETHING FINE
SO FINE, SO FINE, SO FINE

1	
2	
3	
4	Have you ever been on Prozac? I went on Prozac after the birth of me
5	

1	bless him
2	
3	
4	second. Nothing to do with him, bless him. I just went a bit off the rails
5	

47

1

2

3 A bit!   Depression! Christ, I couldn't move

4   Depression   I'd get half way to

5 A bit!

1   I saw a psychiatrist. Plenty

2

3

4 the shops and just stop. Stand there. Hours on end

5

1 to talk about

2

3   Ten years of a crap marriage for starters

4   Dad running off

5

1

2

3   She used to get off her face and bring blokes back

4 Mam drinking

5   Anyone

1   Yes

2

3   Yes

4   Do we really have to drag all this up?

5 she could get her hands on   Yes

1			
2	She was beautiful –		
3		After a fashion	
4			
5			She could've had any man she wanted

1			
2		Couple of nice ones	
3	And she usually did. Some nasty blokes		
4			Lewis
5	And she usually did		Me

1		Was	Hasn't touched a
2		Frances	She got her act together
3			
4			
5	sister's a drinker		

1	drop for over ten years	
2		I was never a drinker
3		Just the Prozac
4		I'm off it now,
5		

1		One of me Mam's – Joey. Folk singer. Had the
2	It's just me and Ella	
3		
4	though	
5		

1 beard but not the belly. Skinny as a pipe cleaner. He used to speak in…
2
3
4
5

1 What were they…those…what do you call them? With the initials…
2
3
4
5

1   That's it. You know the kind of thing: SWALK – 'sealed with a
2
3 Acronyms
4
5

1 loving kiss'. What were some of his…
2
3
4
5   BURMA – be upstairs ready my angel

1   when I come home. What made me think
2   when I come home
3 NORWICH – knickers off ready when I come home
4   when I come home
5   when I come home

1	of him?
2	Who else was there?
3	
4	
5	Tom. Had a really bad tattoo of a shark on

1	
2	
3	Whole house stank of alcohol
4	
5	his chest looked like his biro had leaked

1	
2	
3	and durex
4	
5	

Lights up. Inglewood Police Department.

COP: Officer Hernandez is in Dunkin Donuts when I get the call. He's a big guy, can't function without donuts. They tell me there's some woman singing to herself outside the Sunset Mission Mausoleum down at the cemetery. High on something. Probably a hooker. We got a big problem with prostitution. Last Friday we conducted an anti-prostitution operation along the Manchester Boulevard corridor. I was one of four undercover officers posing as a hooker. We just kinda hang around swinging a handbag. Patent leather. Red patent leather. I think they got a stash of them somewhere. We call this kind of operation a 'John Sting'. I'm very popular with the male Hispanic community. Must be why I married one. We arrested thirteen men. We also impounded their vehicles, which seemed to upset some of them more than the prostitution-related charges. Interesting thing I've noticed, these men are either in their twenties or in their forties. Now if I were a psychologist, which I'm not, I would guess that these guys are either young enough to be unmarried or old enough to be sick of marriage. What does that tell us? I dunno. We have a policy of posting the names of men arrested during John Stings. You can check them on the Department's website. I look for Daniel's name sometimes, my husband. He turned forty a couple of months back.

Lights down.

1		
2	Buried meself in records. 'Ella Swings	
3	I didn't like living at home	
4		
5		

1		'Ella in Berlin'
2	Lightly'	'Ella in Berlin'
3		'Ella in Berlin'
4		'Ella in Berlin'
5	'Ella Fitzgerald – The Cole Porter Songbook' 'Ella in Berlin'	

1	'Mack the Knife'	I loved that	
2		I loved that	
3		I loved that. When Ella forgot the words	
4		I loved that	And she
5		God, I loved that	

1	All the other kids thought I was mad
2	
3	'Don't you
4	just made it up
5	Fantastic

1	'The Bay City Rollers?'
2	
3	like Led Zep?'
4	'Don't you like Deep Purple?'
5	'Mud?'

1	I'd bunk off school and come home –
2	
3	
4	This was when Mam was still working
5	

1	Put a record on top volume and sing along
2	Put a record on top volume and sing along. I used to sing all day
3	
4	Music
5	and sing along

1	
2	I only heard Ella sing live once. It was at
3	
4	going round and round me head
5	

1	
2	the Newport Jazz festival when it was in Middlesbrough. True. At
3	
4	
5	

1	
2	Ayresome Park. Good few years back now. Ella flew in just for the gig.
3	
4	
5	

1	
2	She landed at the airport, got picked up in a limo, driven to the gig,
3	
4	
5	

1	
2	did the gig, got back in the limo and went straight back to the airport.
3	
4	
5	

1	
2	She had another gig somewhere
3	
4	Denmark, I think
5	A piano player I

1	
2	
3	
4	
5	know said he met Tommy Flanagan once, Ella's accompanist in the

1	
2	
3	
4	
5	1970s, Flanagan told him he decided to hand in his notice after

1	
2	
3	
4	
5	they went from Aix-en-Provence to Newcastle-upon-Tyne back to

1	
2	
3	
4	It was just
5	Aix-en-Provence to Wolf Trap, Virginia, in two days

1		
2		
3		Choked on
4	after I saw Ella that me Mam died	Asphyxiation
5	I was 19	

1   When I met Michael I was temping at the Day Centre.

2

3 her own vomit

4

5

---

1 Place for people with learning difficulties. I do a bit of temping now

2

3

4

5

---

1 and then. Bit of extra cash. I used to enjoy working there. There was a

2

3

4

5

---

1 sweet lad called Angus. Had Downs. Lovely nature. He was obsessed

2

3

4

5

---

1 with S Club 7

2   I'd just picked up the kids from me sister's when this Jag

3

4

5

1	Michael	It's raining so
2	pulls up beside us. It's him. Michael	It's raining so
3	Michael	It's raining so
4	Michael	It's raining so
5	Michael. The man in the suit. It's raining so

1	he offers us a lift. I tell him we only live round the corner, but he insists we
2	he offers us a lift. I tell him we only live round the corner, but he insists we
3	he offers us a lift. I tell him we only live round the corner, but he insists we
4	he offers us a lift. I tell him we only live round the corner, but he insists we
5	he offers us a lift. I tell him we only live round the corner, but he insists we

1	get in. So we do. Says he's on his way back down to London. I can't talk.
2	get in. So we do. Says he's on his way back down to London. I can't talk.
3	get in. So we do. Says he's on his way back down to London
4	get in. So we do. Says he's on his way back down to London. I can't talk.
5	get in. So we do. Says he's on his way back down to London

1	I'm mortified. Darren's wiping his Nikes on the	back of the seat. Ali's
2	I'm mortified	back of the seat
3		back of the seat
4	I'm mortified	back of the seat
5		back of the seat

1	dripping all over his camel hair coat. And there's me soaked to the skin
2		camel hair coat
3		camel hair coat
4		camel hair coat
5		camel hair coat

1	in me Asda jeans and one of me ex's Chris de Burgh t-shirts
2	
3	
4	
5	I couldn't've

1	
2	
3	
4	
5	looked less cool if I'd tried

SOMETHING'S GOTTA GIVE

Music & Lyrics: Johnny Mercer

WHEN AN IRRESISTIBLE FORCE

SUCH AS YOU

MEETS AN OLD IMMOVABLE OBJECT LIKE ME

YOU CAN BET AS SURE AS YOU LIVE

SOMETHING GOTTA GIVE

SOMETHING GOTTA GIVE

SOMETHING GOTTA GIVE

WHEN AN IRREPRESSIBLE SMILE

SUCH AS YOURS

WARMS AN OLD IMPLACABLE HEART

SUCH AS MINE

DON'T SAY NO

BECAUSE I INSIST

SOMEWHERE, SOMEHOW, SOMEONE'S GONNA BE KISSED

SO ON GUARD

WHO KNOWS WHAT THE FATES HAVE IN STORE
FROM THEIR VAST MYSTERIOUS SKY
I'LL TRY HARD IGNORING THOSE LIPS I ADORE
BUT HOW LONG CAN ANYONE TRY

Song continues – underscoring.

1			
2	So Ali says to me	And I say	And
3			
4		'Who's that man?'	
5			'Be quiet, darling'

1		'I'm Michael'		'I really like your
2	he says		And then he says	
3			God help us	
4				
5				

1	voice'		'I'm a big jazz fan'	
2		And I'm like	And he says	And I say
3				
4				
5		'Thanks'		

1		'It's not often you hear a really good jazz voice these
2	And he's like	
3		
4		
5	'Me too'	

1	days'	'I love Ella'
2	And then… And then he says	
3		
4	And then he says	
5		

> FIGHT, FIGHT, FIGHT, FIGHT
> FIGHT IT WITH ALL OF OUR MIGHT
> CHANCES ARE SOME HEAVENLY STAR-SPANGLED NIGHT
> YOU'LL FIND OUT
> AS SURE AS WE LIVE
> SOMETHING'S REALLY GOT TO GIVE

Song finishes.

1		Philately will get you nowhere
2		
3	Charlie, me brother, used to collect stamps	
4		
5		

1		
2	S'what Dad used to say	
3		Did you know that a 'dry print' is a stamp with a
4		
5		

1
2
3 weak image on it due to insufficient ink? And that a 'bisect' is a stamp cut in
4
5

1
2
3 half to pay postage at half the rate? This and how to roll a joint are the only
4
5

1
2   Charlie was the
3 useful things me brother ever taught us
4   I'm being unkind
5

1
2 one encouraged us to sing. Always telling us how good I was. Arranged for us
3
4
5

1
2 to do a song with a mate of his at a school concert
3
4   God, I was petrified
5   Did

1 (*Sings.*) HEAVEN, I'M IN HEAVEN

2 I sang 'Cheek to Cheek'

3

4

5 it, though

---

1 AND MY HEART BEATS SO THAT I CAN HARDLY SLEEP, BUT I SEEM

2

3

4 I get very nervous before a gig   Still do   I do

5   Used to   I do not get nervous

---

1 TO FIND THE HAPPINESS I SEEK, WHEN WE'RE OUT TOGETHER

2 I have this routine I go through before I go on. I stand just off-stage,

3

4

5

---

1 DANCING CHEEK TO CHEEK, DANCE WITH ME, I WANT MY ARMS

2 doesn't matter if it's a pub or the Albert Hall

3

4

5   I have sung at the Albert –

---

1 ABOUT YOU –

2

3

4   Miners' benefit

5 I'm trying to speak! Thank you. I have sung at the Albert Hall

1
2   Anyway, before I go on stage I go through the first
3
4   in 1984
5   Quite a night

1
2   number in me head, every word, every intonation
3   Woe betide anyone who
4
5

1
2
3   interrupts   So if
4   I won't go on until I've been right through the song. Can't
5

1
2
3   you see us at the side of the stage before a gig with me eyes shut, talking
4
5

1
2
3   to meself, stay well away
4   There was a girl at school,
5   I do not have a confidence problem

1

2

3

4 Mandy something. Horrible she was. Used to terrorise everyone. She

5

---

1   Michael took

2   She was only 15

3   On acid

4 jumped off the top of the art block

5

---

1 us to Francesca's for a meal, that night, after he picked us up. All of us.

2

3

4

5

---

1 Kids and all. I was praying they'd behave

2

3   They're no angels

4

5   Especially our

1

2   Great sense of irony, though,

3   Drugs

4   Got involved with these lads

5 Darren

1	
2	used to hide their stash round the back of the Law Courts
3	
4	Until the
5	

1	
2	
3	
4	police found it
5	

Lights up. Inglewood Police Department.

COP: Sounds like a routine response, so I decide to leave
    Hernandez – I know better than to come between a man and
    his donuts. It's been a busy day, two robberies, an auto theft
    and two homicides. According to the FBI crime in the City of
    Inglewood decreased for the third consecutive year in 2004.
    You coulda fooled me. I never worked so hard. And I got
    passed over for promotion – again! I get too involved.
    Daniel's always telling me that. I guess that's one of the
    problems – with me and Daniel. He used to work at the Public
    Information Office – he did not get involved. He hated his job.
    So he quit. We're not getting along too well. That's a lie – it's
    hell. I've had it. He drives me crazy; he is so unfocused. All he
    does all day is drink beer and watch TV. It's like being married
    to Homer Simpson. We have not had intimate relations for
    eighteen months. So I'm driving to the cemetery and I promise
    myself tonight I'm gonna tell him…tonight…

Lights down.

1	So we get to talking about Ella
2	I tell him I love the Verve recordings
3	
4	He
5	

1	
2	Stuff from before
3	
4	insists there's a lot of stuff on Decca worth listening to
5	

1	
2	Norman Granz became her manager
3	Rubbish! Such as?
4	
5	There is! The

1	
2	
3	Are you trying to tell me Ellis Larkins is better
4	
5	recordings with Ellis Larkins

1	
2	
3	than Oscar Peterson?
4	Please…Please…Thank you… Michael
5	Ellis Larkins was a fantastic –

1   Asks us about me singing,

2

3

4   says he's got a couple of albums he'll lend us

5

1   me repertoire, me plans

2

3

4

5   He sounds dead serious. Tells us he knows the

1

2   Says he can ask about getting us a

3

4

5   manager of Pizza Express in Soho

1   If I like…?

2   gig if I like

3   I wasn't looking

4   I'm in heaven

5   Why not? I deserve it

1

2

3   for anyone when Michael came along. I was happy enough. I wasn't

4

5

1

2

3 short of cash. What with singing nights at the hotel, cash in hand, and

4

5

1

2   Told us he was an art

3 the job at the Day Centre. I was doing all right

4

5

1

2 dealer. Specialized in mid to late sixteenth century Mannerism and the

3

4

5

1   impressed

2 Baroque   I was impressed

3

4   Michelangelo, Caravaggio   impressed

5   That lot

PRELUDE TO A KISS

Music & Lyrics: Duke Ellington, Irving Gordon & Irving Mills

IF YOU HEAR
A SONG IN BLUE
LIKE A FLOWER CRYING
FOR THE DEW
THAT WAS MY HEART SERENADING YOU
MY PRELUDE TO A KISS

IF YOU HEAR A SONG THAT GROWS
FROM MY TENDER SENTIMENTAL WOES
THAT WAS MY HEART TRYING TO COMPOSE
A PRELUDE TO A KISS

THOUGH IT'S JUST A SIMPLE MELODY
WITH NOTHING FANCY
NOTHING MUCH
YOU COULD TURN IT TO A SYMPHONY
A SCHUBERT TUNE WITH A GERSHWIN TOUCH

OH HOW MY LOVE SONG GENTLY CRIES
FOR THE TENDERNESS WITHIN YOUR EYES
MY LOVE IS A PRELUDE THAT NEVER DIES
A PRELUDE TO A KISS

THOUGH IT'S JUST A SIMPLE MELODY
WITH NOTHING FANCY
NOTHING MUCH
YOU COULD TURN IT TO A SYMPHONY
A SCHUBERT TUNE WITH A GERSHWIN TOUCH

OH HOW MY LOVE SONG SO GENTLY CRIES
FOR THE TENDERNESS WITHIN YOUR EYES
MY LOVE IS A PRELUDE THAT NEVER DIES
A PRELUDE TO A KISS

1	And for a while
2	We fell in love
3	
4	When Dad left us, I was
5	For a while

1	
2	
3	
4	devastated. I could see it was impossible, but you don't think it's going to
5	

1	
2	
3	Then it does
4	happen. Then it does. I don't blame him – Mam on the booze, me and me
5	

1	
2	
3	Never home
4	brother and sister acting up. But he didn't help matters
5	Always

1	
2	
3	Pencil salesman
4	
5	away with his work The things I could tell you about the

1	7B
2	
3	7B. It was an excuse. His work. To stay
4	
5	hardness of pencils – 8H, 7H, 7B…

1	
2	It wasn't
3	away from us No one could be that dedicated to pencils!
4	
5	It was

1	
2	When I was at school I taught meself
3	
4	
5	Mam he was staying away from

1	True
2	to say 'I love you' in eleven different languages I wonder… OK…
3	
4	True
5	

1	
2	Ignoring the easy ones – Je t'aime, and that – there's, Ikh hob dikh lib,
3	
4	
5	

1

2 that's Yiddish. Ya tebya lyublyu, or something like that, Russian. There's,

3

4

5

1

2 oh what was it… Mi amas vin. You'll never guess that one –

3

4

5   Esperanto

1

2 Oh and –

3   Give it a rest

4   Love wasn't something that featured big in my

5

1

2

3   Don't know what I saw

4 marriage. Not after the first year or so, at any rate

5

---

1   Ray   Nice smile

2   Ray   Long legs

3 in him   Ray

4   Ray. Ray

5   Ray. He was a good footballer

1	He had a van

2	Used to take

3	God help us

4	Enormous thumbs	had a van

5	He had a van

1	Blue van

2	us to gigs

3	You can say that

4	Not much of a lover, truth be told

5	Passion wagon

1	

2	

3	again. Not much of an anything

4	

5	I sang at our wedding. As a surprise…

1	

2	Wasn't

3	Was.

4	Wasn't

5	'Let's Call The Whole Thing Off ' – I thought it would be funny

1	

2	

3	Confession. I almost got married once before. When I was 20. Benny

4	

5	

1
2
3 Cornwall. He'd been after us for months. Just kept on at us to marry him.
4
5

1
2
3 In the end I gave in, said I would. Then I find out he's got a criminal
4
5

1
2
3 record as long as... Been banged up four times. History of burglary and
4
5

1
2
3 God knows what. He'd been a fitter in the shipyards. Spent his entire
4
5

1
2
3 redundancy on a hot dog franchise. Went under in six months. Ended
4
5

1

2

3 up owing money to everyone. Some idiot told him I was coming into

4

5

---

1   Me!

2   Me!

3 an inheritance. Me! Anyway, I tell him the engagement's off. I think

4   Me!

5   Me!

1

2

3 he was quite upset, until he found out I didn't have a rich Aunt hidden

4

5

1

2   No, my wedding day wasn't quite what I expected

3 away anywhere

4

5

1

2

3   That's right

4   God yes

5 Ray's best man. Christ… Pissed! Couldn't stand up! Had to push him

1	skateboard	
2		
3	skateboard. Ray thought this was great	
4	skateboard	
5	home on a skateboard	Best moment of the

1		
2		
3		In 1990 a horse called 'Mr Frisk'
4		
5	wedding. Never tired of telling the story	

1	16 to 1
2	
3	won the Grand National. Came in at 16 to 1. I know this because Ray
4	16 to 1
5	16 to 1

1	782 quid. And he spent it	On his mates
2	782 quid	On his mates
3	won – 782 quid	All of it. On his mates
4	782 quid	On his mates
5	782 quid	On his mates

I'M JUST A LUCKY SO AND SO

Lyrics: Mack David　　　　　*Music: Duke Ellington*

AS I WALK DOWN THE STREET

SEEMS EVERYONE I MEET

GIVES ME A FRIENDLY HELLO

It seems i'm just a lucky so and so

The birds in every tree
Are all so neighbourly
They sing wherever i go
It seems i'm just a lucky so and so

If you should ask me the amount
In my bank account
I'd have to confess
That i'm slipping
But that don't worry me
Confidentially
I've got a dream
That's worth living

And when the day is through
Each night i hurry to a home
Where love waits i know
It seems i'm just a lucky so and so

Lights up. Inglewood Police Department.

COP: I drive in the entrance at East Florence Avenue. I park the patrol car by the Elk monument in the Garden of Verses, I don't want her to see the car, and I'm thinking to myself: Yes, I'm gonna do it, I'm gonna ask him for a divorce – tonight! I get out the car, walk over to the Sunset Mission Mausoleum and there she is, just sitting there, singing to herself. She sees me. I'm about to go get her when... There's something about the way she's looking at me. I stop. I think, wait – Procedure. Don't rush in. Appraise the situation. We already had two homicides in the last 24 hours. A security guard and some poor guy that got the back of his head blown off on Century and La Cienega. I don't want me to be number three.

Lights down.

1	
2	If you're ever in LA and you want to visit Ella, you can either take the
3	
4	
5	LA

1	Metro Greenline Shuttle	MTA bus
2	Metro Greenline Shuttle or the	MTA bus. Turn right at the entrance to the
3	Metro Greenline Shuttle	MTA bus
4	Metro Greenline Shuttle	MTA bus
5	Metro Greenline Shuttle	MTA bus

1		Sunset Mission
2	cemetery on Florence Avenue, there in front of you is the	Sunset Mission
3		Sunset Mission
4		Sunset Mission
5		Sunset Mission

1	Mausoleum
2	Mausoleum. Ella is on the second floor. The Sanctuary of the Bells. Crypt
3	Mausoleum
4	Mausoleum
5	Mausoleum

1	
2	1063 – two spaces up from the floor and two spaces in from the doorway on
3	
4	
5	

1	your left	Was. The
2		Was
3	Wasn't worth the effort	
4	Took me a while to find it	Was
5		

1	inscription reads, 'Beloved Mother and Grandmother, Ella Jane Fitzgerald
2	
3	
4	
5	

1	1918 – 1996'
2	
3	And that's it!
4	
5	What about 'The First lady of Song' or 'Jazz

1	
2	She adopted Ray Jnr
3	And another thing, she didn't have any kids
4	
5	Legend'?

1	
2	
3	
4	
5	I thought she'd have this big, I dunno… a proper grave, not one of those

1		hello Ella
2		hello Ella
3		hello Ella. And then this woman comes
4		I say hello Ella.
5	crypt things and a little plaque	hello Ella

1	
2	
3	up to us
4	
5	'Do you know where I can find the crypt for Mayor Tom Bradley?'

1	No		Very	lush
2	No. I go back outside			lush
3	No			lush
4	No	It's very nice, trees, fountains		lush
5			Very green	lush

1	
2	
3	
4	I'm sat there, minding me own business, and then I see her… She's
5	

1	
2	
3	
4	standing a little way off, watching us…
5	

Lights up on COP.

COP: She's staring at me now - real hard…

1		Ella (*To COP.*) Ella…
2		It's Ella (*To COP.*) Ella…
3		Ella (*To COP.*) Ella…
4	It's her…	Ella (*To COP.*) Ella…
5		Ella (*To COP.*) Ella…

COP: Ella?

Lights down. Vamp on 'Mack the Knife'.

1	Thank you, we'd like to do something for you now. We haven't heard a
2	Thank you, we'd like to do something for you now. We haven't heard a
3	Thank you, we'd like to do something for you now. We haven't heard a
4	Thank you, we'd like to do something for you now. We haven't heard a
5	Thank you, we'd like to do something for you now. We haven't heard a

1	girl sing it and since it's so popular we'd like to try and do it for you.
2	girl sing it and since it's so popular we'd like to try and do it for you.
3	girl sing it and since it's so popular we'd like to try and do it for you.
4	girl sing it and since it's so popular we'd like to try and do it for you.
5	girl sing it and since it's so popular we'd like to try and do it for you.

1	We hope we remember all the words…
2	We hope we remember all the words…
3	We hope we remember all the words…
4	We hope we remember all the words…
5	We hope we remember all the words…

Lights back up on COP – she has become Ella.

MACK THE KNIFE

Lyrics: Bertolt Brecht/Marc Blitzstein   *Music: Kurt Weill*

COP: (*Sings.*)

OH, THE SHARK HAS PEARLY TEETH, DEAR
AND HE SHOWS THEM, PEARLY WHITE
JUST A JACK KNIFE HAS MACHEATH, DEAR
AND HE KEEPS IT OUT OF SIGHT

OH, THE SHARK BITES WITH HIS TEETH, DEAR
SCARLET BILLOWS START TO SPREAD
FANCY GLOVES THOUGH, WEARS MACHEATH DEAR
SO THERE'S NOT, NOT A TRACE OF RED

ON A SUNDAY, SUNDAY MORNING
LIES A BODY, OOZIN' LIFE
SOMEONE'S SNEAKING 'ROUND THE CORNER
TELL ME COULD IT BE, COULD IT BE, COULD IT BE
MACK THE KNIFE?

OH, WHAT'S THE NEXT CHORUS?
TO THIS SONG, NOW
THIS IS THE ONE, NOW
I DON'T KNOW
BUT IT WAS A SWINGING TUNE
AND IT'S A HIT TUNE
SO WE TRIED TO DO MACK THE KNIFE

AH, LOUIS MILLER
OH, SOMETHING ABOUT CASH
YEAH, MILLER, HE WAS SPENDING THAT TRASH
AND MACHEATH DEAR, HE SPENDS LIKE A SAILOR
TELL ME, TELL ME, TELL ME

COULD THAT BOY DO, SOMETHING RASH

OH BOBBY DARIN, AND LOUIS ARMSTRONG
THEY MADE A RECORD, OH BUT THEY DID
AND NOW ELLA, ELLA, AND HER FELLAS
WE'RE MAKING A WRECK, WHAT A WRECK
OF MACK THE KNIFE

(*Louis Armstrong imitation.*) OH SNOOKIE TAUDRY, BAH BAH
    BAH NOP DO BO DE DO
BAH BAH BAH NOP DO BO DE DO
JUST A JACK KNIFE HAS MACHEATH, DEAR
AND DO BO BO BAH BAH BAH NOP DO BO DE DO

SO, YOU'VE HEARD IT
YES, WE'VE SWUNG IT
AND WE TRIED TO
YES, WE SUNG IT

YOU WON'T RECOGNIZE IT
IT'S A SURPRISE HIT
THIS TUNE, CALLED MACK THE KNIFE

AND SO WE LEAVE YOU, IN BERLIN TOWN
YES, WE'VE SWUNG OLD MACK
WE'VE SWUNG OLD MACK IN TOWN
FOR THE DARIN FANS,
AND FOR THE LOUIS ARMSTRONG FANS, TOO
WE TOLD YOU LOOK OUT, LOOK OUT, LOOK OUT
OLD MACHEATH'S BACK IN TOWN

Interval

ACT TWO

As at end Act 1.

I'LL BE HARD TO HANDLE

Lyrics: Bernard Dougall   *Music: Jerome Kern*

COP: (*Sings.*)

NOW WE'LL SAY TILL SOMETHING DO US PART
THAT OLD DAD OF MINE AIN'T GOT A HEART
ANY GIRL WHO'S OUT FOR PLEASURE
THINKS OF MARRIAGE ONLY AT HER LEISURE
AS IT IS, THEY'VE GOT THE HORSE BEHIND THE CART

WHEN MY POP SAID WE MUST WED,
HE KIND OF WOWED ME, STILL I'M READ-Y
BUT ONE THING MUST BE CLEAR
AT THIS TIME

I'LL BE HARD TO HANDLE
I PROMISE YOU THAT
AND IF YOU COMPLAIN
HERE'S ONE LITTLE JANE
WHO'LL LEAVE YOU FLAT

I'LL BE HARD TO HANDLE
WHAT ELSE CAN I BE
I SAY WITH A SHRUG
I THINK YOU'RE A MUG
TO MARRY ME

WHEN YOU FIRST THREW ME A GANDER
I WAS WILLING TO PHILANDER
BUT I NEVER THOUGHT I'D HAVE TO BE A BRIDE
NOW YOU'RE GONNA FIND TOUGH SLEDDING

I DON'T WANT NO SHOTGUN WEDDING
I WAS ONLY ALONG FOR THE RIDE

I'LL BE HARD TO HANDLE
I'M TELLING YOU PLAIN
JUST BE A DEAR
AND SCRAM OUT OF HERE
I'M GONNA RAISE CAIN

I'LL BE HARD TO HANDLE
MY BRIDGES ARE BURNED
THIS WEDDING'S A GAG
AND YOU'RE IN THE BAG
WHERE I'M CONCERNED

I'LL BE HARD TO HANDLE
WHEN WE'VE SAID, 'I DO'
SEE THERE'S NO HOPE
I JUST GOT A DOPE
WHEN I TOOK YOU

I'LL BE LIVING MY LIFE IN BED
BUT THEY ALWAYS WILL BE TWIN BEDS
AND I WARN YOU, YOU'LL BE LIVING LIKE A MONK
OUR AFFAIR IS NOW A PAST ONE
SO DON'T THINK YOU'VE PULLED A FAST ONE
JUST REMEMBER, I THINK YOU'RE A PUNK!

I'LL BE HARD TO HANDLE
I'M NO BALL AND CHAIN
I'LL FIND SOME MEANS
TO CALL THE MARINES
I'M GONNA RAISE CAIN
GONNA RAISE CAIN
I'M TELLING YOU PLAIN
I'M GONNA RAISE CAIN

1
2
3 Did you know the Victorians had a set period of mourning for when
4
5

1
2
3 someone died?   If a husband died the period of mourning was
4   True
5

---

1 two and a half years
2 two and a half years
3 two and a half years. When a wife died the period of mourning was
4 two and a half years
5 two and a half years

---

1 three months   Nan told us that
2 three months
3 three months. Does that sound right to you?   Ray used
4 three months
5 three months

1
2
3 to hit us   Idiot
4   We won't dwell on it
5   He used to watch the tele in the bath

1	He was 40	Kids were devastated
2		
3		
4	What a way to go	
5	Electrocuted	

1	
2	It was exactly two and a half years after he died that I met Michael...
3	
4	
5	

1		
2	Period of mourning, see	Fate. Sort of...
3	What?	
4		
5		

Lights up. Inglewood Police Department.

COP: I'm standing there looking at this woman and I want to get this situation over with – quick. But when I try to talk to her, she doesn't make any sense, I mean, she seems to think I'm Ella Fitzgerald. I don't even like Ella Fitzgerald. I tell her – I'm a Police Officer... I'm a Police Officer...

Lights down.

PAUL SIRETT

1	
2	I told
3	
4	
5	Michael always came to hear us sing when he was in Newcastle

1	He told me about him
2	him about me	I discovered he also had a passion
3	
4	
5	

1	
2	for James Bond	*Dr No*
3	James Bond
4	In chronological order
5	Could name all the films

1	*Goldfinger*	Wrong!
2		Wrong!
3	*From Russia With Love*	Wrong!
4	*You Only Live Twice*
5		Wrong!

1	*You Only Live Twice*	Really happy
2	*You Only Live Twice*	I was happy
3	*You Only Live Twice*. Etcetera
4	*You Only Live Twice*
5	*Thunderball*, then *You Only Live Twice*

1
2 He talked about moving his business to the North-East
3
4   Said he was going
5

1
2   I hated it when he was away
3
4 to sell his flat in London   And he went away
5

1   Always rang   Took me with him one
2   Rome   Always
3
4 a lot   Always
5   Amsterdam   Always

1 time
2   Sicily
3
4   He
5   Stayed in the same hotel Winston Churchill had stayed at

1
2   Face went all yellow and
3
4 had an allergic reaction to some fish he'd eaten
5

1		
2	blotchy	
3	Looked like a cheese and tomato pizza	
4		Wouldn't go out
5		

EVERY TIME WE SAY GOODBYE

Music & Lyrics: Cole Porter

EVERY TIME WE SAY GOODBYE
I DIE A LITTLE
EVERY TIME WE SAY GOODBYE
I WONDER WHY A LITTLE
WHY THE GODS ABOVE ME
WHO MUST BE IN THE KNOW
THINK SO LITTLE OF ME
THEY ALLOW YOU TO GO

WHEN YOU'RE NEAR THERE'S SUCH AN AIR OF SPRING ABOUT IT
I CAN HEAR A LARK SOMEWHERE BEGIN TO SING ABOUT IT
THERE'S NO LOVE SONG FINER
BUT HOW STRANGE THE CHANGE FROM MAJOR TO MINOR
EVERY TIME WE SAY GOODBYE

WHEN YOU'RE NEAR THERE'S SUCH AN AIR OF SPRING ABOUT IT
I CAN HEAR A LARK SOMEWHERE BEGIN TO SING ABOUT IT
THERE'S NO LOVE SONG FINER
BUT HOW STRANGE THE CHANGE FROM MAJOR TO MINOR
EVERY TIME WE SAY GOODBYE

1	I was happy	Doing the washing up
2	Really happy. He was so clean	Always taking a
3		Forever changing his
4	And tidy	
5	That cologne he wore	

1	Never stopped	On the phone day and
2	bath	Worked so hard
3	shirt	
4	And his work	
5		

1	night	
2	I didn't mind	I thought I'd been in
3		
4	This was unlike anything…	
5		

1	But this was the real thing	
2	love before	
3		
4	I'd never felt like this	
5	It's	

1	Something good was happening to me
2	I couldn't believe it
3	
4	But it's true
5	a cliché, I know

1	We even talked about going to LA together	
2		
3		
4	To *me!*	
5		To visit Ella's grave

A-TISKET A-TASKET

Music & Lyrics: Traditional

COP: (*Sings.*)

A-TISKET A-TASKET

A GREEN AND YELLOW BASKET

I WROTE A LETTER TO MY LOVE

BUT ON THE WAY I DROPPED IT

I DROPPED IT, I DROPPED IT

AND, ON THE WAY, I DROPPED IT

A LITTLE BOY PICKED IT UP

AND PUT IT IN HIS POCKET

Music continues.

1	I was in love	Beautiful		
2		Hopeless		
3				
4			Impossible	
5				Wonderful

1	love. It was		Really	
2	love	It was		It really was
3				
4	love	It was		
5	love		Quite something	

1	amazing		
2	amazing. Foot massage		
3		He used to give us a foot massage	
4	amazing		
5	amazing		'How are you,

1		'Yes, please'
2		
3		
4		
5	love? Are you tired? Would you like a foot massage?'	'Just

1	'That's right. Fantastic'	He was (*Sighs.*) Ohhhhh…
2		Ohhhhh…
3		
4	As a lover	Ohhhhh…
5	there?'	Ohhhhh…

1		Accomplished…	
2		Very… Accomplished…	
3			
4	Very attentive	Accomplished…	
5		Accomplished…	

COP: (*Sings.*)

A-TISKET A-TASKET

A GREEN AND YELLOW BASKET

I WROTE A LETTER TO MY LOVE

BUT ON THE WAY I DROPPED IT

I DROPPED IT, I DROPPED IT

AND, ON THE WAY, I DROPPED IT

A LITTLE BOY PICKED IT UP

AND PUT IT IN HIS POCKET

Song finishes.

1		He was, wasn't he
2	And he was great with the kids	
3		
4		Generous to a fault
5		

1		God, it was…	
2	Toys		Bliss, man
3			
4	Sweets		
5		Trips to the multiplex	

1	I told him he could stay with us	
2		
3		
4		
5		When he was in Newcastle, like

1	I'd talk about him all the time
2	He agreed
3	Bore people
4	Save on the hotel. He agreed
5	

1	Me and Michael	Michael
2		Michael and Me. Michael, Michael, Michael
3	stiff	Michael, Michael, Michael
4		Michael, Michael
5		Michael, Michael, Michael

1	I'd dedicate songs to him
2	
3	
4	
5	This one's for Michael…

SOMEONE TO WATCH OVER ME

Lyrics: Ira Gershwin   *Music: George Gershwin*

THERE'S AN SAYING OLD, SAYS THAT LOVE IS BLIND
STILL WE'RE OFTEN TOLD, 'SEEK AND YE SHALL FIND'
SO I'M GOING TO SEEK A CERTAIN LAD I'VE HAD IN MIND
LOOKING EVERYWHERE, HAVEN'T FOUND HIM YET
HE'S THE BIG AFFAIR I CANNOT FORGET
ONLY MAN I EVER THINK OF WITH REGRET

I'D LIKE TO ADD HIS INITIAL TO MY MONOGRAM
TELL ME, WHERE IS THE SHEPHERD FOR THIS LOST LAMB?

THERE'S A SOMEBODY I'M LONGIN' TO SEE
I HOPE THAT HE, TURNS OUT TO BE
SOMEONE WHO'LL WATCH OVER ME

I'M A LITTLE LAMB WHO'S LOST IN THE WOOD
I KNOW I COULD, ALWAYS BE GOOD
TO ONE WHO'LL WATCH OVER ME

ALTHOUGH HE MAY NOT BE THE MAN SOME
GIRLS THINK OF AS HANDSOME
TO MY HEART HE CARRIES THE KEY

WON'T YOU TELL HIM PLEASE TO PUT ON SOME SPEED
FOLLOW MY LEAD, OH, HOW I NEED
SOMEONE TO WATCH OVER ME

WON'T YOU TELL HIM PLEASE TO PUT ON SOME SPEED
FOLLOW MY LEAD, OH, HOW I NEED
SOMEONE TO WATCH OVER ME
SOMEONE TO WATCH OVER ME

Lights up. Inglewood Police Department.

COP: So, I'm thinking…okay, crazy woman – I'll take her in, call
the shrink, do the paper work and I can still get home in time
to ask for a divorce. Then she stands up and I see it – a Bren
10mm Autoloading Pistol. Now, I haven't seen one of these
things in, what, ten, fifteen years? Time was everyone wanted
a Bren Ten – it was the Miami Vice thing. Crockett carried
one. So, now I'm thinking…oh shit, it's a crazy woman – with
a gun…

Lights down.

1 Michael tells us he's going away again

2   I'm hoping he

3   Los Angeles

4

5

1

2 might ask us to go with him

3

4   But he doesn't. Says his

5   To see Ella's grave

1

2

3   To LA

4 goodbyes and off he goes   Not to begin with

5   Didn't bother us

1   Said he'd call us when he

2 He was always going away, I've told you that

3

4

5

1 got there (*Pause.*) Nothing

2   (*Pause.*) Nothing   I thought there might have been an

3   (*Pause.*) Nothing

4   (*Pause.*) Nothing. Not a word

5   (*Pause.*) Nothing

1		I rang the airline	
2	an accident		
3		Dead	Flight landed safely
4			
5		I rang his mobile	

1	I was confused	
2		Every night I'd sit by the phone
3		
4		Nothing
5		Days passed

1		I stopped going to work at the Day
2	waiting for him to call	
3		Every night
4		
5		

1	Centre	
2		I didn't bother turning up for gigs
3		doing nothing
4		Just sat at home doing nothing.
5		doing nothing

1	
2	
3	
4	I knew what was happening. I knew the feeling. In me gut. Like a
5	

1	
2	
3	
4	blackness. I couldn't bear it…
5	

'ROUND MIDNIGHT

Music & Lyrics: Thelonius Monk, Cootie Williams & Bernie Hanighen

IT BEGINS TO TELL 'ROUND MIDNIGHT

MIDNIGHT

I DO PRETTY WELL TILL AFTER SUNDOWN

SUPPERTIME I'M FEELING SAD

BUT IT REALLY GETS BAD 'ROUND MIDNIGHT

MEMORIES ALWAYS START 'ROUND MIDNIGHT

HAVEN'T GOT THE HEART TO STAND THOSE MEMORIES

WHEN MY HEART IS FILLED WITH YOU

AND OLD MIDNIGHT KNOWS IT TOO

WHEN A QUARREL WE HAD NEEDS MENDING

DOES IT MEAN THAT OUR LOVE IS ENDING

DARLING I NEED YOU LATELY I FIND

YOU'RE OUT OF MY HEART AND OUT OF MY MIND

LET OUR HEART TAKE WINGS 'ROUND MIDNIGHT

MIDNIGHT

LET THE ANGELS SING FOR YOUR RETURNING

TILL OUR LOVE IS SAFE AND SOUND

AND OLD MIDNIGHT COMES 'ROUND

FEELING SAD

REALLY GETS BAD

'ROUND MIDNIGHT

'ROUND
'ROUND MIDNIGHT

1			So I rang a
2		I had to know what was going on	
3			
4			
5	I decided I had to find him		

1	woman I knew Michael sometimes did business with in London
2	
3	
4	
5	She told us

1			
2		Said he'd rung her Monday	
3	I could've told her that		
4			Monday
5	he was in LA		Monday. Then…

1		I went very quiet	
2			
3	Bombshell		
4			
5		'Why don't you ring his wife?'	'Are you all

1	'Fine'		'What?'	She gives
2				
3				
4				
5	right?'	'Have you got her number?'		'Carlotta…'

1	us the number		
2			Spanish
3		I ring straight away	
4			
5		She sounds Italian	Whatever

1		
2		'I don't give Michael's details out to just
3	Squeaky voice	'I don't give Michael's details out to just
4		
5		Like a mouse. 'I don't give Michael's details out to just

1		I manage to stop meself telling her	how
2	anyone.'		how
3	anyone.'		how
4			how
5	anyone.' Just anyone!		how

1	many times this 'just anyone' has slept with her husband
2	many times this 'just anyone' has slept with her husband
3	many times this 'just anyone' has slept with her husband. Then she says,
4	many times this 'just anyone' has slept with her husband
5	many times this 'just anyone' has slept with her husband

1		And she gives us the number of a gallery out there	
2	'What do I care…'		
3	'What do I care…'		
4	'What do I care…'		
5			

1			
2		Resigned	
3			'I'm afraid Mr Webb
4	She sounded hurt		
5		I ring the number	

1		Tried again	
2			
3	is not available'	'I'm afraid Mr Webb is not available'	
4			
5		Tried again	

1	I try again	And again	And again
2	I try again	And again	And again
3	'He's not here'	'He's not here'	'If you
4		And again	And again
5	I try again	And again	And again

1	So I decide there's only one
2	
3	call one more time I'm going to the police'
4	
5	

1	thing for it
2	
3	
4	
5	I'll go to LA

Lights up. Police Dept.

COP: Shit! Shit! Shit! Shit! Shit! Shit! I'm standing here, no
backup, and there's a crazy woman with a gun looking
straight at me, thinks I'm Ella Fitzgerald. Thank you God!
Now I know I gotta do this by the book, so I take cover and I
press the panic button on my set so the situation goes 'live'.
Then I say, as calmly as I can, 'Put the gun down. There are
other officers on their way...' She doesn't move. Just stands
there, staring at me. I edge my hand to my holster. I say it
again, 'Just put the gun down...' – Nothing!

Lights down.

1	They're broke
2	
3	But I needed some cash
4	So I ask me brother and sister
5	

1	250 quid –
2	All of it
3	As usual
4	I take me jewellery down to Cash Converter
5	

1   the lot!

2

3   I'm not gonna get far on that

4

5   So I go to the hotel where I sing

1

2

3

4   I ask Maggie, the manageress, to lend us some money   But

5   I liked Maggie

---

1   Five

2   No money

3   Bitch

4   she obviously didn't like me

5   So I took her bag

---

1   credit cards   And Goldfish

2   Visa   And 130 quid in cash

3   Egg

4   Virgin

5   Mint

1

2

3   I put her bag back

4

5   She's on the night shift, won't check it for ages

1	I give 200 quid to Frances. Ask her to keep an eye on the kids for us. I get a
2	
3	
4	
5	

1	train to London, straight to Heathrow and I buy a ticket for the next
2	
3	
4	
5	

1	available flight	I'm flying to LA
2		
3		
4		
5	Two hours later	Go to this posh

1	
2	Bath
3	Put on me
4	
5	hotel I see in the in-flight magazine and book meself in

1	
2	
3	make-up
4	
5	

Lights up. Police Dept.

COP: I'm sweating; I can feel it running down my arms and the back of my neck. I say it one more time, 'C'mon honey, put the gun down…nice and slow…c'mon…' She's still staring at me – I mean real intense. And then…then…she smiles… I got my hand on my firearm now and I think, okay lady, any sudden move and you're dead…

Lights down.

1	
2	All kinds of stuff
3	Modern as well as
4	I get a taxi to the gallery
5	Big place

1	I ask after Michael. Tell them I'm his sister. Woman tells me
2	
3	'Baroque'
4	
5	'Baroque'

1	where he's staying. I go there. Apartment block. Press the buzzer
2	
3	
4	
5	

1	I turn around		
2			Getting out of a cab
3		There he is	
4	No answer		
5			

1		'Michael!'	
2		'Michael!'	
3			
4			'Michael!'
5	I wave to him		'Michael!' He sees us

1		Priceless. He comes over	
2		Priceless	'What are you
3	The look on his face – Priceless		
4		Priceless	
5		Priceless	

1		'Michael, what's going on?'	
2	doing here?'		
3		I'm fuming…	
4			'Why didn't you
5			

1		'Why didn't you tell us
2		
3		
4	ring us?'	
5	'What do you think you're playing at?'	

1	you were married?'		he says
2		'Calm down!'	
3			'You've got a lot of explaining
4			
5			

1		'What's going on?'	
2	'Lotte, please, darling –'		'Please, not here…'
3	to do?'	'What's going on?'	
4		'What's going on?'	
5		'What's going on?'	

1		
2		He tells us it's over between him and
3	We go up to his apartment	
4		
5		Very nice

1		
2	Carlotta	They're
3	Tells us it's been over for years	
4		He didn't want to involve us
5		

1		sorry. Really sorry
2	getting a divorce	sorry sorry
3		sorry sorry. He just needed a bit of
4		sorry sorry
5	Tells us he's sorry	sorry

1	
2	He held
3	space
4	Things haven't been going so well lately
5	With the business

1	I was crying
2	me hand He kissed us
3	
4	
5	

BEWITCHED

Music: Richard Rodgers   *Lyrics: Lorenz Hart*

AFTER ONE WHOLE QUART OF BRANDY
LIKE A DAISY I'M AWAKE
WITH NO BROMO SELTZER HANDY
I DON'T EVEN SHAKE

MEN ARE NOT A NEW SENSATION
I'VE DONE PRETTY WELL I THINK
BUT THIS HALF-PINT IMITATION
PUT ME ON THE BLINK

I'M WILD AGAIN
BEGUILED AGAIN
A SIMPERING WHIMPERING CHILD AGAIN
BEWITCHED BOTHERED AND BEWILDERED AM I

COULDN'T SLEEP AND WOULDN'T SLEEP
WHEN LOVE CAME AND TOLD ME I SHOULDN'T SLEEP

BEWITCHED BOTHERED AND BEWILDERED AM I

LOST MY HEART BUT WHAT OF IT
HE IS COLD I AGREE
HE CAN LAUGH BUT I LOVE IT
ALTHOUGH THE LAUGH'S ON ME

I'LL SING TO HIM
EACH SPRING TO HIM
AND LONG FOR THE DAY WHEN I'LL CLING TO HIM
BEWITCHED BOTHERED AND BEWILDERED AM I

HE'S A FOOL AND DON'T I KNOW IT
BUT A FOOL CAN HAVE HIS CHARMS
I'M IN LOVE AND DON'T I SHOW IT
LIKE A BABE IN ARMS

LOVE'S THE SAME OLD SAD SENSATION
LATELY I'VE NOT SLEPT A WINK
SINCE THIS HALF-PINT IMITATION
PUT ME ON THE BLINK

I'VE SINNED A LOT
I'M MEAN A LOT
BUT I'M LIKE SWEET SEVENTEEN A LOT
BEWITCHED BOTHERED AND BEWILDERED AM I

I'LL SING TO HIM
EACH SPRING TO HIM
AND WORSHIP THE TROUSERS THAT CLING TO HIM
BEWITCHED BOTHERED AND BEWILDERED AM I

WHEN HE TALKS HE IS SEEKING
WORDS TO GET OFF HIS CHEST
HORIZONTALLY SPEAKING
HE'S AT HIS VERY BEST

VEXED AGAIN

PERPLEXED AGAIN

THANK GOD I CAN BE OVERSEXED AGAIN

BEWITCHED BOTHERED AND BEWILDERED AM I

Music continues, underscoring.

1	Later, he took us to a restaurant
2	
3	
4	Seafood place. Very exclusive
5	.

1	
2	
3	
4	Then, after the meal, we go for a walk, and he says
5	Fantastic food

1	'I think we should finish it'
2	'I think we should finish it'
3	'I think we should finish it'
4	'I think we should finish it'
5	'I think we should finish it'

1			'I love you'
2	'It's been fun'	'I'm not going back to her'	
3		Fun!	
4	I couldn't speak		
5			

1	'I love you' 'I love you' 'I love you'
2	'I love you' 'I love you'
3	'I love you' 'I love you' 'I love you'
4	Over and over — 'I love you' 'I love you'
5	I say to him — 'I love you' 'I love you'

1	'If you need any money…'
2	'If you need any money…'
3	All he could say was — 'If you need any money…'
4	'If you need any money…'
5	'If you need any money…'

1	'What about us?'
2	'If you need any money…' — 'If you need any money…'
3	
4	
5	

1	'I thought we were in love?'
2	'If you need any money…'
3	And that was it
4	
5	

1	
2	
3	
4	And walked away
5	He called a cab for us

WISE AT LAST

MY EYES AT LAST

ARE CUTTING YOU DOWN TO YOUR SIZE AT LAST

BEWITCHED BOTHERED AND BEWILDERED NO MORE

BURNED A LOT

BUT LEARNED A LOT

AND NOW YOU ARE BROKE SO YOU EARNED A LOT

BEWITCHED BOTHERED AND BEWILDERED NO MORE

COULDN'T EAT

WAS DYSPEPTIC

LIFE WAS SO HARD TO BEAR

NOW MY HEART'S ANTISEPTIC

SINCE YOU MOVED OUT OF THERE

ROMANCE FINIS

YOUR CHANCE FINIS

THOSE ANTS THAT INVADED MY PANTS FINIS

BEWITCHED BOTHERED AND BEWILDERED NO MORE

1	I don't know what put the idea in me head
2	
3	But I knew I was going to kill
4	
5	

1	
2	
3	him
4	
5	

Lights up. Police Dept.

COP: I think I see her hand move…

1	
2	I sat in me hotel room
3	
4	It was just a question of how
5	There and then

1	
2	all the next day
3	Thinking about it
4	The night porter
5	He was from Wisconsin

1	
2	Wore a name badge
3	Percival Aaron Julius
4	'You can call me Julie'
5	Liked

1	I supplied the brandy
2	Familiar
3	Could smell it on him
4	Like Mam
5	a drink

1	
2	
3	Brandy and belch water he called it
4	Tells me his hard
5	Brandy and soda

1	
2	Air marshal
3	Worked at an airport
4	luck story
5	The ones that stand on the

1	He taught us some of the signals…
2	
3	
4	
5	runway, waving those things about

1	
2	(*Demonstrates.*) Means start engines…
3	
4	(*Demonstrates.*) Turn right…
5	

1	He got sacked
2	
3	(*Demonstrates.*) Turn left…
4	
5	(*Demonstrates.*) Slow down…

1	
2	
3	Drunk on the job
4	Directed a 747 backwards into a baggage terminal
5	

1	Lost his house
2	Wife left him
3	
4	
5	Half a million dollars' worth of damage

1	Everything…
2	His savings — Two nights
3	
4	Kept touching us up
5	I didn't care

1	Leered
2	Talked
3	We met — Leered — I take his gun
4	We met — Third night
5	He drank — He passes out

1	I was there ages
2	
3	
4	I wait outside the apartment block for Michael to show
5	

1	
2	Police car drove past
3	Thought they were
4	People giving us funny looks
5	

1	I thought Michael
2	
3	gonna stop
4	I got in a panic
5	Didn't, though. Just kept going

1	wasn't going to show
2	Thought maybe he'd gone
3	Back to England
4	I felt dizzy
5	

1	
2	Then I saw
3	
4	I was breathing funny. Me heart beating like I don't know what
5	

1	He didn't see us
2 him	
3 And I felt calm	
4	He was waiting for a cab
5	He crouched

1	
2	And when he did
3	
4	I walked up
5 down to get something out of his briefcase	

1	In the back of the head
2	In the back of the head
3 And I shot him	
4 behind him…	In the back of the head
5	In the back of the head

COP: (*Shouts.*) 'Put the Motherfucking gun down!'… I can see she's crying. And then…then she says…

1 'I killed him'	
2 'I killed him'	
3 'I killed him'	
4 'I killed him'	
5 'I killed him'	

COP: 'Who?'

1	'Michael'
2	'Michael'
3	'Michael'
4	'Michael'
5	'Michael'

COP: 'Michael? Who – When was this?'

1	'Today'
2	'Today'
3	'Today'
4	'Today'
5	'Today'

COP: 'Where?'

1	'I don't know. Someplace…'
2	'I don't know. Someplace…'
3	'I don't know. Someplace…'
4	'I don't know. Someplace…'
5	'I don't know. Someplace…'

COP: 'On Century and La Cienega?'

1	'I don't know. I got a bus here. To the cemetery. To see you…'
2	'I don't know. I got a bus here. To the cemetery. To see you…'
3	'I don't know. I got a bus here. To the cemetery. To see you…'
4	'I don't know. I got a bus here. To the cemetery. To see you…'
5	'I don't know. I got a bus here. To the cemetery. To see you…'

COP: 'I am not Ella Fitzgerald.'

HOW HIGH THE MOON

Music & Lyrics: Morgan Lewis & Nancy Hamilton

COP: (*Sings.*)

SOMEWHERE THERE'S MUSIC
HOW FAINT THE TUNE
SOMEWHERE THERE'S HEAVEN
HOW HIGH THE MOON
THERE IS NO MOON ABOVE
WHEN LOVE IS FAR AWAY TOO
TILL IT COMES TRUE
THAT YOU LOVE ME AS I LOVE YOU

SOMEWHERE THERE'S MUSIC
HOW NEAR, HOW FAR
SOMEWHERE THERE'S HEAVEN
IT'S WHERE YOU ARE
THE DARKEST NIGHT WOULD SHINE
IF YOU WOULD COME TO ME SOON
UNTIL YOU WILL, HOW STILL MY HEART
HOW HIGH THE MOON

SOMEWHERE THERE'S MUSIC
HOW FAINT THE TUNE
SOMEWHERE THERE'S HEAVEN
HOW HIGH THE MOON
THE DARKEST NIGHT WOULD SHINE
IF YOU WOULD COME TO ME SOON
UNTIL YOU WILL, HOW STILL MY HEART
HOW HIGH THE MOON

Scat solo, into crescendo of voices – music continues.

1	
2	I loved him
3	
4	Why did I do it?
5	They

1	Please…	Be quiet…	Be quiet…
2	I loved him	He was so good to me	So good
3	Why? Why?	He used us! He was a bastard!	
4	Why did I do it? Why, why, why…	I am evil… Evil bitch… Sick…	
5	can't blame me He asked for it!	They can't do anything	

1	Please, enough… Stop it… I can't listen to this… Leave me alone… Please
2	So kind… All the things he did for me… All the lovely things… I loved him…
3	He was like all men! He deserved it! Do you hear me? He deserved it! He
4	Sick… What kind of person… I didn't deserve him. I wasn't good enough
5	to me. It was his fault. Everything! I never did any wrong. Nothing! Not a

1	leave me alone… Stop it… Stop… Stop it… STOP IT!	Stop… Stop…
2	Now what do I do… I never loved anyone like I loved –	Stop… Stop…
3	was a nasty, manipulative bastard! Don't ever forget –	Stop… Stop…
4	for him. I wasn't good enough. I hope they kill me, I –	Stop… Stop…
5	thing. I was in the right. They'll see that. I was in the –	Stop… Stop…

1	Stop… Stop… STOP!
2	Stop… Stop… STOP!
3	Stop… Stop… STOP!
4	Stop… Stop… STOP!
5	Stop… Stop… STOP!

Music stops. Silence.

COP: She puts the gun on the ground. I go over… I move the
firearm out of reach. I cuff her.

---

1 Michael's dead…

2 Michael's dead…

3 Michael's dead…

4 Michael's dead…

5 Michael's dead…

COP: Two patrol cars arrive. Hernandez shows – all 265 lbs of
him, huffin' and a-puffin'. 'What's happening?' I tell him I'll
explain later. We get her in the car; bring her back here. I take
her to the detention facility, check her things – watch, dark
glasses, CD walkman. She tells me her story. It's something
else…

---

1 I have asked for four other offences to be taken into consideration…

2

3   The

4

5

1

2

3 murder of Amanda Linda Gallagher, by pushing from a tall building, when

4

5

1	
2	
3	I was fifteen
4	The murder of my mother, Jane Elizabeth Hanway, by
5	

1	
2	The murder of my husband, Raymond
3	
4	asphyxiation, when I was nineteen
5	

1	
2	Leslie William Phillips, by electrocution, when I was thirty-nine
3	
4	
5	The murder

1	
2	
3	
4	
5	of Percival Aaron Julius, security guard at the Orlando Hotel, Los Angeles,

1	also by asphyxiation
2	also by asphyxiation
3	also by asphyxiation
4	also by asphyxiation
5	also by asphyxiation

COP: I gotta see if her story checks out. It's gonna take a while. I'm gonna be late… for Daniel. What the hell. This is big. I can ask for a divorce some other time…

She picks up LOTTE's CD Walkman, puts the headphones on and presses 'Play'.

MISS OTIS REGRETS

Music & Lyrics: Cole Porter

MISS OTIS REGRETS SHE'S UNABLE TO LUNCH TODAY, MADAM
MISS OTIS REGRETS SHE'S UNABLE TO LUNCH TODAY
SHE IS SORRY TO BE DELAYED, BUT LAST EVENING DOWN IN LOVERS' LANE, SHE STRAYED, MADAM
MISS OTIS REGRETS SHE'S UNABLE TO LUNCH TODAY

WHEN SHE WOKE UP AND FOUND THAT HER DREAM OF LOVE WAS GONE, MADAM
SHE RAN TO THE MAN WHO HAD LED HER SO FAR ASTRAY
AND FROM UNDER HER VELVET GOWN, SHE DREW A GUN AND SHOT HER LOVER DOWN, MADAM
MISS OTIS REGRETS SHE'S UNABLE TO LUNCH TODAY

WHEN THE MOB CAME AND GOT HER AND DRAGGED HER FROM THE JAIL, MADAM
THEY STRUNG HER UP ON THAT WILLOW ACROSS THE WAY
AND THE MOMENT BEFORE SHE DIED, SHE LIFTED UP HER LOVELY HEAD AND CRIED, MADAM
MISS OTIS REGRETS SHE'S UNABLE TO LUNCH TODAY

YES, THE MOMENT BEFORE SHE DIED, SHE LIFTED UP HER LOVELY HEAD AND CRIED, MADAM
MISS OTIS REGRETS SHE'S UNABLE TO LUNCH TODAY

End

www.ingramcontent.com/pod-product-compliance
Ingram Content Group UK Ltd.
Pitfield, Milton Keynes, MK11 3LW, UK
UKHW031252020325
455690UK00007B/89